QUEEN

GREATEST PIX II

**IMP
BOOKS**

First published in Great Britain in 1991
by International Music Publications.

© 1991 Queen Productions Ltd
under exclusive licence to
International Music Publications.

ISBN 0 86359 807 2

Printed in Great Britain by Panda Press

International Music Publications
Woodford Trading Estate
Southend Road
Woodford Green
Essex IG8 8HN

IMP
BOOKS

QUEEN

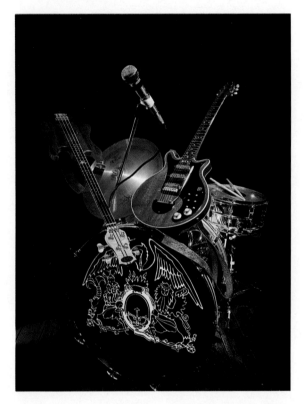

GREATEST PIX II

COMPILED AND DESIGNED BY
RICHARD GRAY

PHOTOGRAPHS BY : DAVID BAILEY, PAUL COERTEN, SIMON FOWLER, RICHARD GRAY,
PETER HINCE, GEORGE HURRELL, CLARE MULLER, DENIS O'REGAN, NEAL PRESTON,
PAUL RIDER, PETER RÖSHLER, TORLEIF SVENSSON AND RICHARD YOUNG.

A KIND OF MAGIC VIDEO, PLAYHOUSE THEATRE, LONDON, 1986

THE HOT SPACE TOUR, 1982

RADIO GA GA VIDEO, 1984

THE WORKS TOUR, 1984

ROGER TAYLOR, MAN ON FIRE VIDEO, 1984

METROPOLIS STUDIOS, LONDON, 1991

THE WORKS TOUR, 1984

THE WORKS TOUR, 1984

ROCK IN RIO, 1985

ROCK IN RIO, 1985

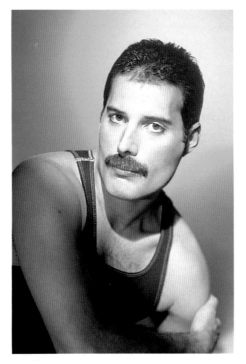

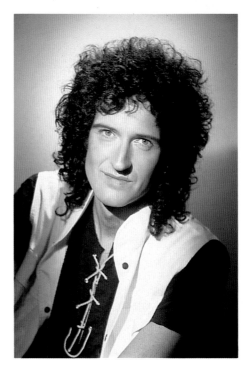

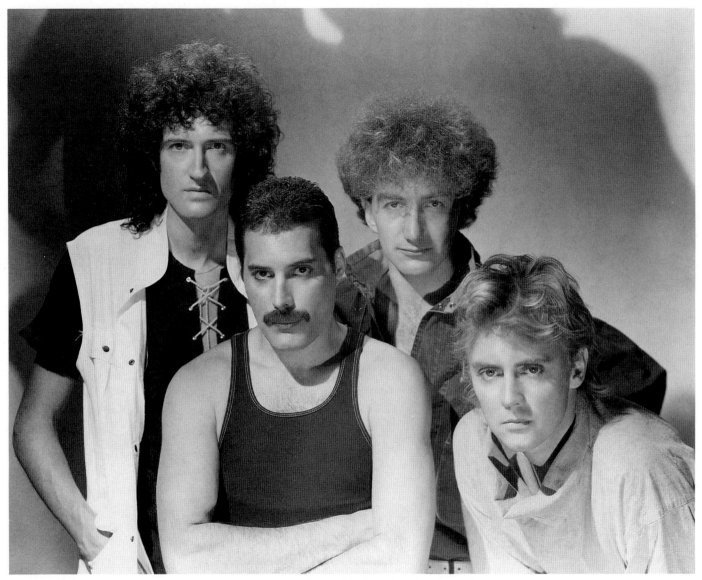

THE WORKS, LOS ANGELES, 1983

THE MAGIC TOUR, 1986

ONE VISION VIDEO, MUSICLAND STUDIOS, MUNICH, 1985

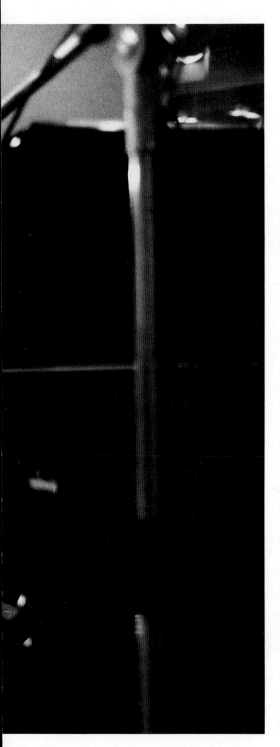

ONE VISION VIDEO, MUSICLAND STUDIOS, MUNICH, 1985

ROCK IN RIO, 1985

LIVE AID, 1985

It's A Hard Life video, Munich, 1984

LIVE AID, WEMBLEY, LONDON, 1985

LIVE AID, JULY 13ᵀᴴ 1985

WHO WANTS TO LIVE FOREVER video, London, 1986

ONE VISION VIDEO, MUSICLAND STUDIOS, MUNICH, 1985

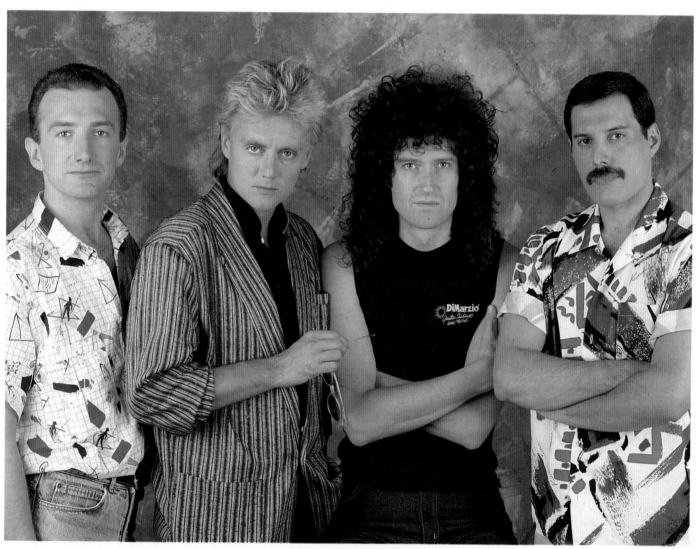

THE COMPLETE WORKS, 1985

◄ THE WORKS TOUR, 1984

39

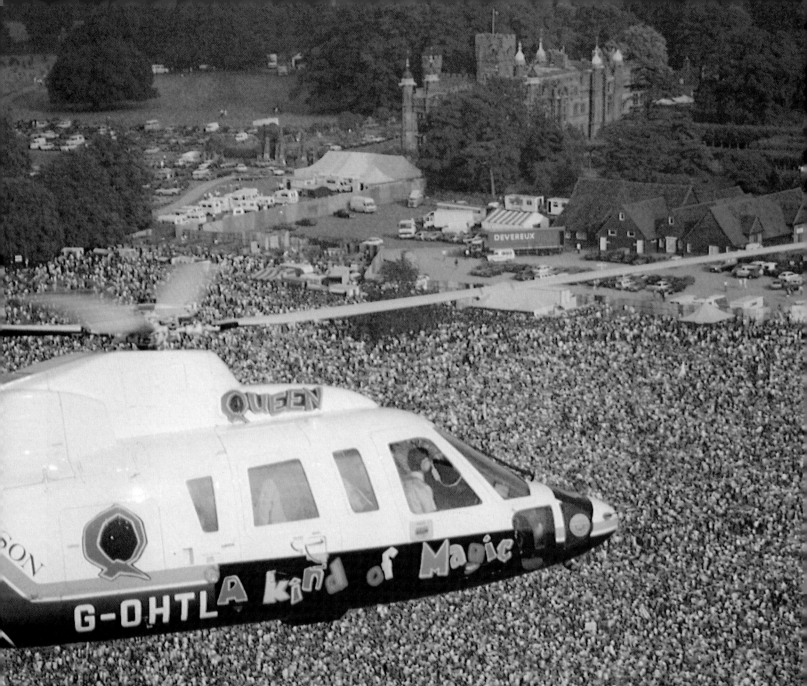

◄ THE MAGIC TOUR, KNEBWORTH, 1986

THE MAGIC TOUR, 1986

THE MAGIC TOUR,
KNEBWORTH,
AUGUST 9TH 1986 ▶

FREDDIE MERCURY, THE GREAT PRETENDER VIDEO, 1987. WITH ROGER TAYLOR AND PETER STRAKER

FREDDIE MERCURY AND MONTSERRAT CABALLÉ, BARCELONA VIDEO, 1987

THE INVISIBLE MAN VIDEO, PINEWOOD STUDIOS, 1989

THE INVISIBLE MAN, 1989

I Want To Break Free video, 1984

I Want To Break Free video, 1984

I WANT TO BREAK FREE VIDEO, LIMEHOUSE STUDIOS, LONDON, 1984

THE MAGIC TOUR, SLANE CASTLE, DUBLIN, 1986

THE MAGIC TOUR, 1986

BREAKTHRU VIDEO, NENE VALLEY RAILWAY, CAMBRIDGESHIRE, 1989

BREAKTHRU VIDEO, 1989

THE WORKS TOUR, 1984

THE MIRACLE, OLYMPIC STUDIOS, LONDON, 1989

BRIAN MAY, AFTER PERFORMING WITH DEF LEPPARD AT THE FORUM, LOS ANGELES, 1983

I Want It All video, Elstree Studios, 1989

I WANT IT ALL VIDEO, 1989

PRINCES OF THE UNIVERSE VIDEO, WITH CHRISTOPHER LAMBERT, 1986

THE MAGIC TOUR, 1986

I'M GOING SLIGHTLY MAD VIDEO, 1991

I'M GOING SLIGHTLY MAD VIDEO, 1991

I'M GOING SLIGHTLY MAD VIDEO, 1991

HEADLONG VIDEO, METROPOLIS STUDIOS, LONDON, 1991

HEADLONG VIDEO, METROPOLIS STUDIOS, LONDON, 1991

SCANDAL VIDEO, PINEWOOD STUDIOS, 1989

THE MIRACLE VIDEO, ELSTREE STUDIOS, 1989

FRIENDS WILL BE FRIENDS VIDEO, LONDON, 1986

◄ THE MAGIC TOUR, SLANE CASTLE, DUBLIN, 1986

METROPOLIS STUDIOS, LONDON, 1991

ROGER TAYLOR WITH THE CROSS, 1990

92

PRINCES OF THE UNIVERSE VIDEO, 1986

OLYMPIC STUDIOS, LONDON, 1989

QUEEN ARE : FREDDIE MERCURY, BRIAN MAY, ROGER TAYLOR AND JOHN DEACON.

MANAGEMENT : JIM BEACH.

PUBLICITY : SCOTT RISEMAN LIPSEY MEADE PR, 22 STEPHENSON WAY, LONDON NW1 2HD.

QUEEN INTERNATIONAL FAN CLUB : 46 PEMBRIDGE ROAD, LONDON W11 3HN.

SPECIAL THANKS TO JULIE GLOVER AND JIM JENKINS.

ALSO AVAILABLE :
QUEEN GREATEST HITS II - THE ALBUM AND QUEEN GREATEST FLIX II - THE VIDEO